W9-AOY-982

Contents

Apples grow from **seeds**.

Harvesttime

Apples

By Inez Snyder

Welcome
Books™

Children's Press®
A Division of Scholastic Inc.
New York / Toronto / London / Auckland / Sydney
Mexico City / New Delhi / Hong Kong
Danbury, Connecticut

Photo Credits: Cover © Sheldon Collins/Corbis; p. 5 © Photodisc; p. 7 © Bohemian Nomad Picturemakers/Corbis; p. 9 © Craig Tuttle/Corbis; p. 11 © James P. Blair/Corbis; p. 13 © Josef Scaylea/Corbis; p. 15 © Bradley Smith/Corbis; p. 17 © Paul Seheult; Eye Ubiquitous/Corbis; p. 19 © Ed Lallo/Index Stock Imagery, Inc.; p. 21 © Corbis

Contributing Editors: Jennifer Silate and Shira Laskin
Book Design: Erica Clendening

Library of Congress Cataloging-in-Publication Data

Snyder, Inez.
    Apples / by Inez Snyder.
    p. cm. — (Harvesttime)
    Summary: Simple text introduces the process of growing and harvesting apples.
    ISBN 0-516-27595-X (lib. bdg.) — ISBN 0-516-25910-5 (pbk.)
    1. Apples—Juvenile literature. 2. Apples—Harvesting—Juvenile literature. [1. Apples. 2. Apples—Harvesting.] I. Title. II. Series.

SB363.S68 2003
634'.11—dc22

                                                                2003014450

Apple seeds grow into trees.

Apple trees can grow
very tall.

7

Some apples turn red when they are ready to be **harvested**.

Most apples are ready to be picked in the **fall**.

9

Apple pickers **climb** ladders to reach the apples.

11

Apple pickers pick the apples carefully.

They do not want to **bruise** the apples.

After the apples are picked, they are put on a truck.

The truck will take the apples to a **warehouse**.

At the warehouse, people pack the apples in boxes.

17

The boxes of apples are sent to stores.

People can buy apples at the stores.

RED
DELICIOUS
$1.19
LB

19

Many people like to eat apples.

New Words

bruise (**brooz**) to make a dark mark on something by dropping or hitting it

climb (**klime**) to move up something using your hands and feet

fall (**fawl**) the season between summer and winter

harvested (**hahr**-vuhst-uhd) picked or gathered

seeds (**seedz**) the parts of plants that can grow in soil and make new plants

warehouse (**wair**-hous) a large building used for storing goods

To Find Out More

Books

How Do Apples Grow?
by Betsy C. Maestro
HarperCollins Children's Books

Picking Apples and Pumpkins
by Amy Hutchings
Scholastic Inc.

Web Site
Just for Kids
http://www.bestapples.com/kids/
Learn about apples, what animals eat them, and play
fun games on this Web site.

Index

apple pickers,
   10, 12

bruise, 12

climb, 10

fall, 8

harvested, 8

ladders, 10

seeds, 4, 6

stores, 18

warehouse, 16

About the Author

Inez Snyder has written several books to help children learn to read. She also enjoys cooking for her family.

Reading Consultants

Kris Flynn, Coordinator, Small School District Literacy, The San Diego County Office of Education

Shelly Forys, Certified Reading Recovery Specialist, W.J. Zahnow Elementary School, Waterloo, IL

Paulette Mansell, Certified Reading Recovery Specialist, and Early Literacy Consultant, TX

24